The Jesus Prayer Rosary

Michael Cleary SVD is parish priest of
St Mary-on-the-Quay Church in Bristol

The Jesus Prayer Rosary

*Biblical Meditations for
Praying with Beads*

Michael Cleary SVD

CANTERBURY
PRESS
Norwich

© Michael Cleary SVD 2007

First published in 2007 by the Canterbury Press Norwich
(a publishing imprint of Hymns Ancient & Modern Limited,
a registered charity)
13–17 Long Lane, London ECIA 9PN

www.scm-canterburypress.co.uk

British Library Cataloguing in Publication data

A catalogue record for this book is available
from the British Library

ISBN 978–1–85311–811–1

Typeset by Regent Typesetting
Printed and bound by
Biddles Ltd, King's Lynn, Norfolk

Contents

To my very dear friend
Sister Geraldine Knightly S.Sp.S.
in memory of our time together
in Wroughton.

Introduction

Lots of people have come to know and use the Jesus Prayer. Lots of people are also coming to value praying with beads. The Jesus Prayer rosary brings the two together. During the many stages of its preparation, the Jesus Prayer rosary has been used in ecumenical as well as Roman Catholic settings. It has been much appreciated – even, remarkably, by those who have always been uncomfortable with any kind of rosary, no matter the amount of special pleading to which they were subjected.

One of our more lively young altar servers was told recently that I was writing a book about Jesus that would help the boy stop his mind from wandering at Mass. Well, I very much doubt that this is that book. But what he was told was right enough. Concentrating on Jesus is what this little work is all about. It's also a pretty good description of what Christians down the years have called 'meditation'. Making it possible for people to do so, in a way that changes their lives, is what they have called 'evangelization'. At least, that's the way St Paul understood it: 'For it is the God who said, "Let light shine out of darkness", who has shone in our hearts to give the light of the knowledge of the glory of God in the face of Christ' (2 Corinthians 4.6). And, staying focused on that face is for the apostle the secret of the spiritual life, the life of transforming grace: 'beholding the glory of the Lord, [we] are being changed into his likeness from one degree of glory to another; for this comes from the Lord who is the Spirit' (2 Corinthians 3.18).

We could call the Jesus Prayer rosary an exercise in staying focused using New Testament texts. There are four sets of meditations on the person and work of Christ, as these are understood by the New Testament writers. We follow them, as it were, as they 'ponder these things' (Luke 2.19). We have episodes from the infancy stories of Matthew and Luke. Then there are scenes from the ministry of Jesus, his passion and death. Finally, in the fifth set of meditations, the New Testament writers give us insight into our experience of him as the Risen One, transforming our lives and in the end taking us to himself, in the heart of the Father.

Readings have been selected for the meditations. As there is more than one way of looking at things in the New Testament, sometimes passages from more than one author are suggested for a particular meditation (see, for instance, the meditations on the crucifixion and death of Jesus). This means that in the case of public/group prayer, some preparation will need to be done, texts chosen beforehand and shared out. The shorter readings, indicated by ❖, are particularly suitable for private use, and may even be memorized for praying while out walking, or waiting for a bus!

One of the oldest and most popular methods for concentrating on Jesus is the Jesus Prayer: 'Jesus, Lord and Christ, Son and Word of the Living God, have mercy (on me a sinner/us sinners)'.[1] As its name implies, the Jesus Prayer rosary makes use of this ancient repetitive formula in response to the scripture readings. With its roots in Eastern Christianity,[2] the Jesus Prayer is now used by a great many people, whatever their Christian tradition. *The Catechism of the Catholic Church* encourages its use, and sums up very well what it's all about: 'To pray "Jesus" is to invoke him and to call him within us. His name is the only one that contains the presence it signifies. Jesus is the Risen One, and whoever invokes the name of Jesus is welcoming the Son of God who loved him and who gave himself up for him.'[3] A version of the Jesus Prayer is prayed ten times as an integral part of each meditation. It includes what is best called a 'Jesus clause'. Again, think of the altar boy! It's a cunning ploy to keep us focused. A theme, suggested by the scripture reading, is maintained by repeatedly making reference to it.[4] So, for example, while meditating on the death of Jesus:

> Jesus, Lord and Christ,
> Son and Word of the Living God:
> **you passed from this world to the Father,**
> **have mercy (on us).**

Sometimes the clause is even more striking when the petition for mercy is left implied rather than said. In the case of the meditations on the infancy, the ministry, and life in Christ, it may even be more appropriate to replace it altogether by 'we give you thanks and praise'.

Our sisters and brothers in the Orthodox Churches often recite the Jesus Prayer on a prayer rope usually containing 100 knots; sometimes on a cord of beads.[5] To some people, this way of praying seems rather odd, to say the least. Why do you need to *count* your prayers anyway? For whose benefit are you repeating words, like some magical incantation? Aren't you stifling the spontaneity that comes from the Spirit? Didn't Jesus have something to say against thinking we will be heard because of our 'many words' (Matthew 6.7)? Well, the use of prayer-counters, if we can call them that, is for nobody's benefit but our own. It's a simple and effective way of structuring one's prayer; and structure is what we all need, because we live in space and time, and time is not our own. It's a simple and uncomplicated way of saying: 'Whether in the company of others or alone, I will sit here for such-and-such an amount of time (a round of beads, say). This time will be given over to focusing on Jesus (with whatever spontaneity that might surprisingly produce). I will use this time, silently pondering his image as it comes across to me in scripture. I will use this time, speaking to him in my own words and in words I have made my own. I will do what the psalmist does, and repeat myself over and over again with words of praise and adoration[6], or, like poor Bartimaeus, with cries for help.[7] Jesus doesn't need to hear these words. I need to say them. That way, they might sink in!' Structure is what it's all about. Structure is unavoidable! It's an essential condition for any act of worship, even the kind that rejects appointed liturgy books. And it helps to keep our minds from wandering. We may go off into some daydream, but sooner or later the icon in front of which we are praying, the liturgical drama unfolding before us, the book in our hands, the string of beads passing through our fingers, will gently and powerfully call us back to reality.

For nearly a thousand years (it's difficult to say with

any precision), Roman Catholics have used a form of bead-prayer, a way of remembering Jesus, that has evolved into what we know today as 'the Rosary of the Blessed Virgin Mary'.[8] We have chosen to use it as the model for the Jesus Prayer rosary principally because it is the most common arrangement of prayer-beads available, and its method has over the centuries brought all kinds of spiritual enrichment to literally millions of people.[9] It continues to do so, and is now valued as a form of prayer by people of more than one Christian tradition.[10] A section, Appendix 1, is provided in this book for those who would still like to use the Hail Mary as the prayer's characteristic element. Different readings, however, with other themes than those associated with the traditional Marian rosary, have been used. They may be seen in the sections called Meditations on the Infancy According to St Matthew and Meditations on Life in Christ, and in Appendix 3: Other Meditations.

By far the most enjoyable part of this work for me has been the selection of the Concluding Prayers for each meditation.[11] Old personal favourites have been used, as well as newly discovered ones. For the major part they are taken from liturgical sources; hence the almost constant use of the plural form. But experience has shown that they can have a powerful impact when, in private prayer, the single form is used instead. The purpose of the Concluding Prayers is to sum up the theme (or *a* theme) of the reading. Thus, in the last and great meditation on the heavenly Jerusalem, in a prayer obviously inspired by St Augustine,[12] we pray that we may be drawn to the Creator and be brought 'at last to your heavenly city where we shall see you face to face'; a fitting place to end, in every sense.

Michael Cleary SVD
Parish Priest of St Mary-on-the-Quay
Roman Catholic Church, Bristol
Easter 2007

Notes

1 This arrangement emphasizes the name by placing it first. The exaltation titles 'Lord' and 'Christ' recall the resurrection Christology of Acts 2.36. 'Son of the Living God' is from the great Petrine Confession at Matthew 16.16 – itself very possibly a faith declaration rooted in the Easter experience (see 1 Corinthians 15.5; Luke 24.34). 'Word' refers us to the Christology of the Prologue of the Fourth Gospel (John 1.14), where it indicates God being personally and visibly present in the person and work of Jesus. The plea for mercy recalls the story of Blind Bartimaeus (Mark 10.46–52).

2 Kallistos Ware, 'The Origins of the Jesus Prayer', in *The Study of Spirituality*, ed. C. Jones, G. Wainwright, E. Yarnold (London: SPCK, 1986), pp. 175–84.

3 *The Catechism of the Catholic Church,* revised edition (London: Geoffrey Chapman, 1999), no. 2666. See also no. 2667.

4 In Appendix 1, provision has been made for the same practice when the 'Hail Mary' is used.

5 John D. Millar, *Beads & Prayers: The Rosary in History & Devotion* (London: Burns & Oates, Continuum, 2002), pp. 91–2.

6 Psalm 136, but also Psalms 46, 67, 80, 118, 136, 150.

7 'Many sternly ordered him to keep quiet, but he cried out even more loudly, "Son of David, have mercy on me!"' (Mark 10.48).

8 Millar, *Beads & Prayers,* pp. 7–32.

9 A powerful testimony to this is the work of jazz singer and writer, Liz Kelly, *The Seeker's Guide to the Rosary* (Chicago: Loyola Press, 2001).

10 Austin Farrer (Anglican), *Lord I Believe* (London: SPCK, 1962), ch. IX 'The Heaven-sent Aid'; Robert Llewelyn (Anglican), *A Doorway to Silence: the Contemplative Use of the Rosary* (London: Darton, Longman & Todd, 1986); J. Neville Ward (Methodist), *Five for Sorrow, Ten for Joy* (London: Darton, Longman & Todd, 1993); Anthony Price (Anglican), *Reconsidering the Rosary* (Nottingham: Grove Books, 1991). Then there are the following websites:

Orthodox Christians and the rosary: <http://www.unicorne. org/orthodoxy/hiver2004/prayer.htm.>

The popularity of the prayer among some Protestants: <http:// www.recordonline.com/archive/2005/02/05/cover05.htm>

11 The concluding prayer is always best said by one person. Often people may prefer to replace the concluding prayer with one or two verses from a hymn relative to the meditation.

12 'Christ says, "No one can come to me unless drawn by the Father" (Jn. 6.44). Do not think that you are drawn against your will. The mind is also drawn by love . . . Some might say, "How can I believe with the will if I am 'drawn'?" ' I say . . . you are drawn by delight. What is it to be drawn by delight? The psalmist says "Delight yourself in the Lord, and he will give you the desires of your heart" (Ps. 37.4) . . . We are drawn to Christ when we delight in happiness, delight in being just, delight in everlasting life; for all of these are found in Christ . . . Give me someone that loves. Such a one will know what I mean. Give me someone who longs, who hungers, who knows what it is to travel in this wilderness thirsting and panting after the fountain of our eternal home. Give me someone like that. Such a one will understand. But if I speak to the cold and indifferent, they will not understand' (Augustine, Homily on the Gospel of John, 26, 4; PL 35, nos. 1607–09).

The Round of Beads

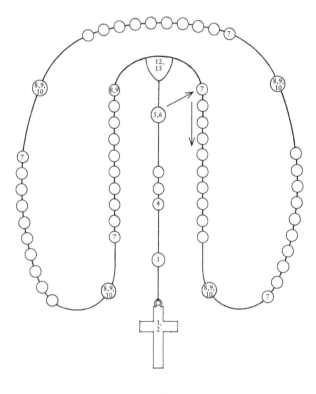

How to Pray the Jesus Rosary

1 We adore you, O Christ, and we bless you.
  Because by your holy cross you have redeemed the
  world

2 Holy God,
  Holy and strong,
  Holy and immortal,
  have mercy on us.

3 Pray the Lord's Prayer.

4 On the next three beads, say the following:

  (i) Jesus, son of David, have pity on me.
  (ii) You are the Christ, the Son of the living God.
  (iii) Jesus Christ is Lord,
      to the glory of God the Father.

5 Pray the 'Glory Be . . .'

6 Having announced the **title** of the first meditation, read the **scripture** passage, **meditate**, and then pray the **Lord's Prayer**.

7 Pray the **Jesus Prayer** on each of the ten beads.

8 Pray the 'Glory Be . . .'

9 Pray the **Concluding Prayer** (in group/public prayer, this should be said by one person).

10 Having announced the **title** of the next meditation, read the **scripture** passage, **meditate**, and then pray the **Lord's Prayer**.

11 Repeat Steps 7 to 10 until all the meditations are complete.

12 On the Centrepiece, recite one of the **Centrepiece Prayers** (pp. 76–82).

13 A **Concluding Prayer** (examples on pages 87–89)

At the Beginning of Each Set of Meditations

1 While holding the cross or crucifix, say:

We adore you, O Christ, and we bless you.
Because by your holy cross you have redeemed the world

Holy God,
Holy and strong,
Holy and immortal,
have mercy on us.

2 On the first single bead, say the Lord's Prayer.

3 On the next three beads, say the following words:

(i) **Jesus, son of David, have pity on me.**
(ii) **You are the Christ, the Son of the living God.**
(iii) **Jesus Christ is Lord,**
     to the glory of God the Father.

4 Then announce the title of the set of meditations to follow.

Meditations on the Infancy According to St Matthew

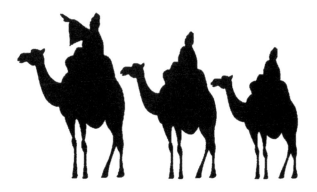

For each Meditation:
Announce the title of the Meditation.
Read the Scripture text.
Pause for reflection.
Say the Lord's Prayer on the single bead.
Say the Jesus Prayer on each of the ten beads.
Say the Glory be to the Father . . .
Say the Concluding Prayer.

1 The Annunciation to Joseph, Son of David

Now the birth of Jesus the Messiah took place in this way. When his mother Mary had been engaged to Joseph, but before they lived together, she was found to be with child from the Holy Spirit. Her husband Joseph, being a righteous man and unwilling to expose her to public disgrace, planned to dismiss her quietly. But just when he had resolved to do this, an angel of the Lord appeared to him in a dream and said, 'Joseph, son of David, do not be afraid to take Mary as your wife, for the child conceived in her is from the Holy Spirit. She will bear a son, and you are to name him Jesus, for he will save his people from their sins.' All this took place to fulfil what had been spoken by the Lord through the prophet:

'Look, the virgin shall conceive and bear a son,
and they shall name him Emmanuel',

which means, 'God is with us.' When Joseph awoke from sleep, he did as the angel of the Lord commanded him; he took her as his wife, but had no marital relations with her until she had borne a son and he named him Jesus.

(Matthew 1.18–25)

4

✤ Joseph, son of David, do not be afraid to take Mary as your wife, for the child conceived in her is from the Holy Spirit. She will bear a son, and you are to name him Jesus, for he will save his people from their sins.

Jesus Prayer
Jesus, Lord and Christ,
Son and Word of the Living God:
you are the work of the Holy Spirit,
have mercy (on us).

Concluding Prayer
Almighty God,
who called Joseph to be the husband of the Virgin
   Mary,
and the guardian of your only Son:
open our eyes and our ears
to the messages of your holy will,
and give us the courage to act upon them;
through Jesus Christ our Lord.[1]

2 The Visit of the Magi

In the time of King Herod, after Jesus was born in Bethlehem of Judea, wise men from the East came to Jerusalem, asking, 'Where is the child who has been born king of the Jews? For we observed his star at its rising, and have come to pay him homage.' When King Herod heard this, he was frightened, and all Jerusalem with him; and calling together all the chief priests and scribes of the people, he inquired of them where the Messiah was to be born. They told him, 'In Bethlehem of Judea; for so it has been written by the prophet:

"And you, Bethlehem, in the land of Judah,
  are by no means least among the rulers of Judah;
for from you shall come a ruler
  who is to shepherd my people Israel."'

Then Herod secretly called for the wise men and learned from them the exact time when the star had appeared. Then he sent them to Bethlehem, saying, 'Go and search diligently for the child; and when you have found him, bring me word so that I may also go and pay him homage.' When they had heard the king, they set out; and there, ahead of them, went the star that they had seen at its rising, until it stopped over the place where the child was. When they saw that the star had stopped, they were overwhelmed with joy. On entering the house, they saw the child with Mary his mother; and they knelt down and paid him homage. Then, opening their treasure-chests, they offered him gifts of gold, frankincense, and myrrh. And having been warned in a dream not to return to Herod, they left for their own country by another road.

(Matthew 2.1–12)

❖ After Jesus was born in Bethlehem of Judea, wise men from the East came to Jerusalem, asking, 'Where is the child who has been born king of the Jews? For we observed his star at its rising, and have come to pay him homage.'

Jesus Prayer
Jesus, Lord and Christ,
Son and Word of the Living God:
you are the desire of the nations,
have mercy (on us).

Concluding Prayer
O God,
by the leading of a star,
you manifested your only Son to the peoples of the
    earth.

Lead us, who know you now by faith,
to your holy presence,
where we may see your glory face to face;
through Jesus Christ your Son our Lord,
who is alive and reigns with you
in the unity of the Holy Spirit,
one God for ever and ever. Amen.[2]

3 The Escape into Egypt[3]

Now after [the wise men from the East] had left, an
angel of the Lord appeared to Joseph in a dream and
said, 'Get up, take the child and his mother, and flee
to Egypt, and remain there until I tell you; for Herod
is about to search for the child, to destroy him.' Then
Joseph got up, took the child and his mother by night,
and went to Egypt, and remained there until the death
of Herod. This was to fulfil what had been spoken by
the Lord through the prophet, 'Out of Egypt I have
called my son.'

(Matthew 2.13–15)

Jesus Prayer
Jesus, Lord and Christ,
Son and Word of the Living God:

you were destined to be a sign
rejected by many,[4]
have mercy (on us).

Concluding Prayer
Almighty God,
in response to your word,
Joseph the son of David
brought the Messiah to the gentiles
when he took Jesus with his mother into the land of
    Egypt.

Grant that we too in answer to your call,
may rise and bring Christ to others;
for he is our Risen Lord
who reigns with you in the unity of the Holy Spirit,
one God for ever and ever. Amen.[5]

4 The Massacre of the Male Infants

When Herod saw that he had been tricked by the wise
men, he was infuriated, and he sent and killed all the
children in and around Bethlehem who were two years
old or under, according to the time that he had learned

from the wise men. Then was fulfilled what had been spoken through the prophet Jeremiah:

'A voice was heard in Ramah,
wailing and loud lamentation,
Rachel weeping for her children;
she refused to be consoled, because they are no
    more.'

(Matthew 2.16–18)

❖ 'A voice was heard in Ramah,
wailing and loud lamentation,
Rachel weeping for her children;
she refused to be consoled, because they are no
    more.'

Jesus Prayer
Jesus, Lord and Christ,
Son and Word of the Living God:
you lived under the sign of persecution,[6]
have mercy (on us).

Concluding Prayer
Heavenly Father,
whose children suffered at the hands of Herod,

though they had done no wrong:
give us grace
neither to act cruelly
nor to stand indifferently by,
but to defend the weak from the tyranny of the
    strong;
in the name of Jesus Christ who suffered for us,
but is alive and reigns with you and the Holy Spirit,
one God, now and for ever. Amen.[7]

5 The Return

When Herod died, an angel of the Lord suddenly appeared in a dream to Joseph in Egypt and said, 'Get up, take the child and his mother, and go to the land of Israel, for those who were seeking the child's life are dead.' Then Joseph got up, took the child and his mother, and went to the land of Israel. But when he heard that Archelaus was ruling over Judea in place of his father Herod, he was afraid to go there. And after being warned in a dream, he went away to the district of Galilee. There he made his home in a town called Nazareth, so that what had been spoken through the prophets might be fulfilled, 'He will be called a Nazorean.'

(Matthew 2.19–23)

Jesus Prayer
Jesus, Lord and Christ,
Son and Word of the Living God:
you deliver us,
and lead us into freedom,
have mercy (on us).

Concluding Prayer
God our redeemer,
you call us into freedom,
just as long ago you called your son Israel[8]
out of the house of slavery.

Grant that we may follow Jesus,
the leader of our salvation,[9]
and so come at last to the land you promise,
where he lives and reigns with you
in the unity of the Holy Spirit,
one God for ever and ever. Amen.[10]

At the centrepiece, recite one of the following: **Jesus,**
Saviour of the World, *the* **Song of Zechariah** *(Luke*
1.68–79), **Mary's Song of Praise** *(Luke 1.46–55), the*
Song of Simeon *(Luke 2.29–32).*

Meditations on the Infancy
According to St Luke

For each Meditation:
Announce the title of the Meditation.
Read the Scripture text.
Pause for reflection.
Say the Lord's Prayer on the single bead.
Say the Jesus Prayer on each of the ten beads.
Say the Glory be to the Father . . .
Say the Concluding Prayer.

1 The Annunciation to Mary

In the sixth month the angel Gabriel was sent by God to a town in Galilee called Nazareth, to a virgin engaged to a man whose name was Joseph, of the house of David. The virgin's name was Mary. And he came to her and said, 'Greetings, favoured one! The Lord is with you.' But she was much perplexed by his words and pondered what sort of greeting this might be. The angel said to her, 'Do not be afraid, Mary, for you have found favour with God. And now, you will conceive in your womb and bear a son, and you will name him Jesus. He will be great, and will be called the Son of the Most High, and the Lord God will give to him the throne of his ancestor David. He will reign over the house of Jacob for ever, and of his kingdom there will be no end.' Mary said to the angel, 'How can this be, since I am a virgin?' The angel said to her, 'The Holy Spirit will come upon you, and the power of the Most High will overshadow you; therefore the child to be born will be holy; he will be called Son of God. And now, your relative Elizabeth in her old age has also conceived a son; and this is the sixth month for her who was said to be barren. For nothing will be impossible with God.' Then Mary said, 'Here am I, the servant of the Lord; let it be with me according to your word.' Then the angel departed from her.

(Luke 1.26–38)

❖ The Holy Spirit will come upon you, and the power of the Most High will overshadow you; therefore the child to be born will be holy; he will be called Son of God . . . Mary said, 'Here am I, the servant of the Lord; let it be with me according to your word.' Then the angel departed from her.

Jesus Prayer
Jesus, Lord and Christ,
Son and Word of the Living God:
you are the work of the Holy Spirit,
have mercy (on us).

Concluding Prayer
By accepting your Word, O God, at the message of an angel, Mary was filled with the light of the Holy Spirit and became your chosen dwelling place. Following her example, may we always be ready to hear your word and keep it with sincerity. We ask this through Jesus Christ, your Son our Lord, who dwells with you in glory with the Holy Spirit, one God for ever and ever. Amen.[11]

or:

We beseech you, O Lord,
pour your grace into our hearts
that as we have known the incarnation of your Son
   Jesus Christ
by the message of an angel,
so by his cross and passion
we may be brought to the glory of his resurrection;
through Jesus Christ your Son our Lord,
who is alive and reigns with you,
in the unity of the Holy Spirit,
one God, now and for ever.[12]

2 The Visit of Mary to Elizabeth

In those days Mary set out and went with haste to a Judean town in the hill country, where she entered the house of Zechariah and greeted Elizabeth. When Elizabeth heard Mary's greeting, the child leapt in her womb. And Elizabeth was filled with the Holy Spirit and exclaimed with a loud cry, 'Blessed are you among women, and blessed is the fruit of your womb. And why has this happened to me, that the mother of my Lord comes to me? For as soon as I heard the sound of your greeting, the child in my womb leapt for joy. And blessed is she who believed that there would be a fulfilment of what was spoken to her by the Lord.'

And Mary said,

'My soul magnifies the Lord,
and my spirit rejoices in God my Saviour.'

(Luke 1.39–47)

❖ And Elizabeth was filled with the Holy Spirit and exclaimed with a loud cry, 'Blessed are you among women, and blessed is the fruit of your womb. And why has this happened to me, that the mother of my Lord comes to me? For as soon as I heard the sound of your greeting, the child in my womb leapt for joy. And blessed is she who believed that there would be a fulfilment of what was spoken to her by the Lord.' . . . And Mary said, 'My soul magnifies the Lord, and my spirit rejoices in God my Saviour'.

Jesus Prayer
Jesus, Lord and Christ,
Son and Word of the Living God:
you visit us like the dawn from on high,[13]
have mercy (on us).

Mighty God,
by whose grace Elizabeth rejoiced with Mary
and greeted her as the mother of the Lord:
look with favour on your lowly servants
that, with Mary, we may magnify your holy name
and rejoice to acclaim her Son our Saviour,
who is alive and reigns with you,
in the unity of the Holy Spirit,
one God, now and for ever. Amen.[14]

3 The Birth of Jesus

In those days a decree went out from Emperor Augustus that all the world should be registered. This was the first registration and was taken while Quirinius was governor of Syria. All went to their own towns to be registered. Joseph also went from the town of Nazareth in Galilee to Judea, to the city of David called Bethlehem, because he was descended from the house and family of David. He went to be registered with Mary, to whom he was engaged and who was expecting a child. While they were there, the time came for her to deliver her child. And she gave birth to her firstborn son and wrapped him in bands of cloth, and laid him in a manger, because there was no place for them in the inn.

In that region there were shepherds living in the fields, keeping watch over their flock by night. Then an angel of the Lord stood before them, and the glory of the Lord shone around them, and they were terrified. But the angel said to them, 'Do not be afraid; for see – I am bringing you good news of great joy for all the people: to you is born this day in the city of David a Saviour, who is the Messiah, the Lord. This will be a sign for you: you will find a child wrapped in bands of cloth and lying in a manger.' And suddenly there was with the angel a multitude of the heavenly host, praising God and saying,

'Glory to God in the highest heaven,
and on earth peace among those he favours!'

When the angels had left them and gone into heaven, the shepherds said to one another, 'Let us go now to Bethlehem and see this thing that has taken place, which the Lord has made known to us.' So they went with haste and found Mary and Joseph, and the child lying in the manger. When they saw this, they made known what had been told them about this child; and all who heard

it were amazed at what the shepherds told them. But
Mary treasured all these words and pondered them in
her heart. The shepherds returned, glorifying and praising God for all they had heard and seen, as it had been
told them.

(Luke 2.1–20)

❖ 'Do not be afraid; for see – I am bringing you good
news of great joy for all the people: to you is born
this day in the city of David a Saviour, who is the
Messiah, the Lord. This will be a sign for you: you
will find a child wrapped in bands of cloth and lying
in a manger'.

Jesus Prayer
Jesus, Lord and Christ,
Son and Word of the Living God:
you became flesh and dwelt among us,
have mercy (on us)

Concluding Prayer
Almighty and everlasting God,
who stooped to raise fallen humanity
through the child-bearing of blessed Mary:
grant that we, who have seen your glory

revealed in our human nature,
and your love made perfect in our weakness,
may daily be renewed in your image
and conformed to the pattern of your Son,
Jesus Christ our Lord,
who is alive and reigns with you,
in the unity of the Holy Spirit,
one God, now and for ever. Amen.[15]

4 The Presentation of Jesus in the Temple

When the time came for their purification according to the law of Moses, they brought him up to Jerusalem to present him to the Lord (as it is written in the law of the Lord, 'Every firstborn male shall be designated as holy to the Lord'), and they offered a sacrifice according to what is stated in the law of the Lord, 'a pair of turtle-doves or two young pigeons.'

Now there was a man in Jerusalem whose name was Simeon; this man was righteous and devout, looking forward to the consolation of Israel, and the Holy Spirit rested on him. It had been revealed to him by the Holy Spirit that he would not see death before he had seen the Lord's Messiah. Guided by the Spirit, Simeon came into the temple; and when the parents brought in the child Jesus, to do for him what was customary under the law, Simeon took him in his arms and praised God, saying,

'Master, now you are dismissing your servant in
    peace,
    according to your word;
for my eyes have seen your salvation,
    which you have prepared in the presence of all
    peoples,
a light for revelation to the Gentiles
    and for glory to your people Israel.'

And the child's father and mother were amazed at what was being said about him. Then Simeon blessed them and said to his mother Mary, 'This child is destined for the falling and the rising of many in Israel, and to be a sign that will be opposed so that the inner thoughts of many will be revealed – and a sword will pierce your own soul too.'

There was also a prophet, Anna the daughter of Phanuel, of the tribe of Asher. She was of a great age, having lived with her husband for seven years after her marriage, then as a widow to the age of eighty-four. She never left the temple but worshipped there with fasting and prayer night and day. At that moment she came,

and began to praise God and to speak about the child to
all who were looking for the redemption of Jerusalem.

(Luke 2.22–38)

❖ Simeon took [the child Jesus] in his arms and
praised God . . . And [Anna] began to praise God,
and to speak about the child to all who were looking
for the redemption of Jerusalem.

Jesus Prayer
Jesus, Lord and Christ,
Son and Word of the Living God:
you are light for the gentiles
and glory for your people Israel,[16]
have mercy (on us)

Concluding Prayer
Almighty Father,
whose Son Jesus Christ was presented in the Temple
and acclaimed the glory of Israel
and the light of the nations:
grant that in him we may be presented to you
and in the world may reflect his glory;
through Jesus Christ our Lord.[17]

5 The Finding of the Boy Jesus in the Temple

Now every year his parents went to Jerusalem for the festival of the Passover. And when he was twelve years old, they went up as usual for the festival. When the festival was ended and they started to return, the boy Jesus stayed behind in Jerusalem, but his parents did not know it. Assuming that he was in the group of travellers, they went a day's journey. Then they started to look for him among their relatives and friends. When they did not find him, they returned to Jerusalem to search for him. After three days they found him in the temple, sitting among the teachers, listening to them and asking them questions. And all who heard him were amazed at his understanding and his answers. When his parents saw him they were astonished; and his mother said to him, 'Child, why have you treated us like this? Look, your father and I have been searching for you in great anxiety.' He said to them, 'Why were you searching for me? Did you not know that I must be in my Father's house?' But they did not understand what he said to them.

(Luke 2.41–50)

❖ 'Why were you searching for me? Did you not know that I must be in my Father's house?'

Jesus Prayer
Jesus, Lord and Christ,
Son and Word of the Living God:
**you were found in your Father's house,
have mercy (on us).**

Concluding Prayer
Heavenly Father,
whose incarnate Son was found to be
wholly dedicated to your will:
grant that in all things we may be found in your
    service
and so come at length to behold the beauty of your
    Temple,
where you live and reign with your Son
in the power of the Holy Spirit,
one God for ever and ever. Amen.[18]

At the centrepiece, recite one of the following: **Jesus,
Saviour of the World,** *the* **Song of Zechariah** *(Luke
1.68–79),* **Mary's Song of Praise** *(Luke 1.46–55), the*
Song of Simeon *(Luke 2.29–32).*

Meditations on the Ministry

For each Meditation:
Announce the title of the Meditation.
Read the Scripture text.
Pause for reflection.
Say the Lord's Prayer on the single bead.
Say the Jesus Prayer on each of the ten beads.
Say the Glory be to the Father . . .
Say the Concluding Prayer.

1 The Baptism of Jesus

In those days Jesus came from
Nazareth of Galilee and was
baptized by John in the Jordan.
And just as he was coming up
out of the water, he saw the
heavens torn apart and the
Spirit descending like a dove
on him. And a voice came from

heaven, 'You are my Son, the Beloved; with you I am well pleased.'

(Mark 1.9–11)

❖ And John testified, 'I saw the Spirit descending from heaven like a dove, and it remained on him. I myself did not know him, but the one who sent me to baptize with water said to me, "He on whom you see the Spirit descend and remain is the one who baptizes with the Holy Spirit." And I myself have seen and have testified that this is the Son of God'.

(John 1.32–34)

Jesus Prayer
Jesus, Lord and Christ,
Son and Word of the Living God:
**you were anointed with the Holy Spirit
and with power,**[19]
have mercy (on us).

Concluding Prayer
God, Creator and Redeemer,
at his baptism in the Jordan,
your voice was heard over the waters,
calling Jesus your beloved Son
while your Spirit decended upon him,
anointing him for service.

May your Spirit descend
and remain with us
your beloved sons and daughters,
created anew in the waters of baptism.

May we thereby follow in the steps of your Son
and spend our lives in the service of your Kingdom.

We ask this in his name. Amen.[20]

2 The Glory of Jesus revealed in the Wine Miracle at Cana

On the third day there was a wedding at Cana in
Galilee. The mother of Jesus was there, and Jesus and
his disciples had also been invited. And they ran out
of wine, since the wine provided for the feast had all
been used, and the mother of Jesus said to him, 'They
have no wine.' Jesus said, 'Woman, what do you want
from me? My hour has not come yet.' His mother said
to the servants, 'Do whatever he tells you.' There were
six stone water jars standing there, meant for the ablu-
tions that are customary among the Jews: each could
hold twenty or thirty gallons. Jesus said to the ser-

vants, 'Fill the jars with water,' and they filled them to the brim. Then he said to them, 'Draw some out now and take it to the president of the feast.' They did this; the president tasted the water, and it had turned into wine. Having no idea where it came from, though the servants who had drawn the water knew, the president of the feast called the bridegroom and said, 'Everyone serves good wine first and the worse wine when the guests are well wined; but you have kept the best wine till now.'

This was the first of Jesus' signs: it was at Cana in Galilee. He revealed his glory, and his disciples believed in him.

(John 2.1–11, NJB)

❖ 'Everyone serves good wine first and the worse wine when the guests are well wined; but you have kept the best wine till now.' . . . [Jesus] revealed his glory, and his disciples believed in him.

Jesus Prayer
Jesus, Lord and Christ,
Son and Word of the Living God:
you changed the water into wine,
have mercy (on us).

Concluding Prayer

Almighty God, the giver of strength and joy,

whose Son turned the water into wine at Cana in
  Galilee:

change our bondage into liberty,

and the poverty of our nature into the riches of your
  grace;

that by the transformation of our lives your glory
  may be revealed;

through Jesus Christ our Lord.[21]

3 Jesus Proclaims the Coming of the Kingdom

When John [the Baptist] heard in prison what the Messiah was doing, he sent word by his disciples and said to him, 'Are you the one who is to come, or are we to wait for another?' Jesus answered them, 'Go and tell John what you hear and see: the blind receive their sight, the lame walk, the lepers are cleansed, the deaf hear, the dead are raised, and the poor have the good news brought to them. And blessed is anyone who takes no offence at me.'

(Matthew 11.2–6)

or:

When [Jesus] came to Nazareth, where he had been brought up, he went to the synagogue on the Sabbath day, as was his custom. He stood up to read, and the scroll of the prophet Isaiah was given to him. He unrolled the scroll and found the place where it is written:

> 'The Spirit of the Lord is upon me, because he has anointed me to bring good news to the poor. He has sent me to proclaim release to the captives and recovery of sight to the blind, to let the oppressed go free, to proclaim the year of the Lord's favour.'

And he rolled up the scroll, gave it back to the attendant and sat down. The eyes of all the synagogue were fixed on him. Then he began to say to them, 'Today this scripture has been fulfilled in your hearing.' All spoke well of him and were amazed at the gracious words that came from his mouth.

(Luke 4.16–22a)

❖ Now after John was arrested, Jesus came to Galilee, proclaiming the good news of God, and saying, 'The time is fulfilled, and the kingdom of God has come near; repent, and believe in the good news.'

(Mark 1.14–15)

Jesus Prayer
Jesus, Lord and Christ,
Son and Word of the Living God:
**you heal the broken-hearted,
and bind up all their wounds,**[22]
have mercy (on us).

Concluding Prayer
Out of your power and compassion, O God,
you sent your Son into our afflicted world
to proclaim the day of salvation.
Heal the broken-hearted;
bind up our wounds.
Bring us health of body and spirit
and raise us to new life in your service.

We make our prayer through our Lord Jesus Christ
who lives and reigns with you in the unity of the
    Holy Spirit,
God for ever and ever. Amen.[23]

4 The Transfiguration of Jesus

[Jesus said to his disciples] 'I tell you truly, there are some standing here who will not taste death before they see the kingdom of God.'

Now about eight days after this had been said, he took with him Peter, John and James and went up the mountain to pray. And it happened that, as he was praying, the aspect of his face was changed and his clothing became sparkling white. And suddenly there were two men talking to him; they were Moses and Elijah appearing in glory, and they were speaking of his passing which he was to accomplish in Jerusalem. Peter and his companions were heavy with sleep, but they woke up and saw his glory and the two men standing with him. As these were leaving him, Peter said to Jesus, 'Master, it is wonderful for us to be here; so let us make three shelters, one for you, one for Moses and one for Elijah.' He did not know what he was saying. As he was saying this, a cloud came and covered them with shadow; and when they went into the cloud the disciples were afraid. And a voice came from the cloud saying, 'This is my Son, the Chosen One. Listen to him.'

(Luke 9.27–35, NJB)

❖ [Jesus] received honour and glory from God the Father when that voice was conveyed to him by the Majestic Glory, saying 'This is my Son, my Beloved, with whom I am well pleased.' We ourselves heard this voice come from heaven, while we were with him on the holy mountain.

(2 Peter 1.17–18)

Jesus Prayer
Jesus, Lord and Christ,
Son and Word of the Living God:
you were revealed in glory
on the holy mountain,
have mercy (on us).

Concluding Prayer
Heavenly Father,
in the transfiguration of Jesus on the holy mountain
you gave his chosen disciples
a vision of the glory that lay before him
in his passion, death and resurrection.

You overshadowed them
with the cloud of your Presence.[24]

They heard your voice
bidding them listen to Jesus your beloved Son
as the one who fulfils the Law and the Prophets.

May your Holy Spirit overshadow us
so that, while being obedient to his word,
we too may see in Jesus the radiance of your glory.[25]

May we so contemplate him on the holy mountain
that we will come to share in his transfiguration,
being transformed by your Holy Spirit
into his image, from one degree of glory to
    another.[26]

We make this prayer through Christ
whom you raised into glory
by the power of your life-giving Spirit.
Amen.[27]

5 The Last Supper

For the tradition I received from the Lord and also handed on to you is that on the night he was betrayed, the Lord Jesus took some bread, and after he had given thanks, he broke it, and he said, 'This is my body, which is for you; do this in remembrance of me.' And in the same way, with the cup after supper, saying, 'This cup is the new covenant in my blood. Whenever you drink it, do this as a memorial of me.' Whenever you eat this bread, then, and drink this cup, you are proclaiming the Lord's death until he comes.

(1 Corinthians 11.23–26, NJB)

❖ [Jesus] took bread, and when he had given thanks, he broke it and gave it to them, saying, 'This is my body given for you; do this in remembrance of me.'

He did the same with the cup after supper, and said,
'This cup is the new covenant in my blood poured
out for you.'

(Luke 22.19–20, NJB)

Jesus Prayer
Jesus, Lord and Christ,
Son and Word of the Living God:
you make yourself known to us
in the breaking of bread,[28]
have mercy (on us).

Concluding Prayer
Father, we give you thanks and praise.

By the work of your Holy Spirit:
we, who eat the bread that is broken
and drink the cup that is blessed,[29]
receive the redeeming Christ.

When we renew the memory of his passion
our minds are filled with grace
and you give us a pledge of future glory.

Father, we give you thanks and praise.[30]

At the centrepiece, recite one of the following: **Jesus, Saviour of the World**, the **Song of Zechariah** *(Luke 1.68–79)*, **Mary's Song of Praise** *(Luke 1.46–55)*, the **Song of Simeon** *(Luke 2.29–32)*.

Meditations on the Passion

For each Meditation:
Announce the title of the Meditation.
Read the Scripture text.
Pause for reflection.
Say the Lord's Prayer on the single bead.
Say the Jesus Prayer on each of the ten beads.
Say the Glory be to the Father . . .
Say the Concluding Prayer.

1 Jesus Prays in Gethsemane

They went to a place called Gethsemane; and he said to his disciples, 'Sit here while I pray.' He took with him Peter and James and John, and began to be distressed and agitated. And he said to them, 'I am deeply grieved, even to death; remain here, and keep awake.' And going a little farther, he threw himself on the ground and prayed that, if it were possible, the hour might pass from him. He said, 'Abba, Father, for you all things are possible; remove this cup from me; yet, not what I want, but what you want.' He came and found them sleeping; and he said to Peter, 'Simon, are you asleep? Could you not keep awake one hour? Keep awake and pray that you may not come into the time of trial; the spirit indeed is willing, but the flesh is weak.' And again he went away and prayed, saying the same words. And once more he came and found them sleeping, for their eyes were very heavy; and they did not know what to say to him. He came a third time and said to them, 'Are you still sleeping and taking your rest? Enough! The hour has come; the Son of Man is betrayed into the hands of sinners. Get up, let us be going. See, my betrayer is at hand.'

(Mark 14.32–42)

❖ 'Father, if you are willing, remove this cup from me; yet, not my will but yours be done.'

(Luke 22.44)

Jesus Prayer
Jesus, Lord and Christ,
Son and Word of the Living God:
**you abandoned yourself
to the will of the Father,
have mercy (on us).**

Concluding Prayer
Take, Lord, and receive all my liberty, my memory, my understanding and my entire will – all that I have and call my own. You have given it all to me. To you, Lord, I return it. Everything is yours; do with it what you will. Give me only your love and your grace. That is enough for me.[31]

2 The Betrayal and Arrest of Jesus

Immediately, while [Jesus] was still speaking, Judas, one of the twelve, arrived; and with him there was a crowd with swords and clubs, from the chief priests, the scribes, and the elders. Now the betrayer had given them a sign, saying, 'The one I will kiss is the man; arrest him and lead him away under guard.' So when he came, he went up to him at once and said, 'Rabbi!' and kissed him. Then they laid hands on him and arrested him.

(Mark 14.43–46)

❖ 'Judas, dost thou betray the Son of man with a kiss?' (Luke 22.48).

Jesus Prayer
Jesus, Lord and Christ,
Son and Word of the Living God:
**you were given up into the hands of sinners,
have mercy (on us).**

Concluding Prayer
Almighty Father,
look with mercy on this your family
for which our Lord Jesus Christ was content to be
  betrayed
and given up into the hands of sinners
and to suffer death upon the cross;
who is alive and glorified with you and the Holy
  Spirit,
one God, now and for ever.[32]

3 The Soldiers Mock Jesus

So Pilate, wishing to satisfy the crowd, released Barabbas for them; and after flogging Jesus, he handed him over to be crucified.

Then the soldiers led him into the courtyard of the palace (that is, the governor's headquarters); and they called together the whole cohort. And they clothed him in a purple cloak; and after twisting some thorns into a crown, they put it on him. And they began saluting him, 'Hail, King of the Jews!' They struck his head with a reed, spat upon him, and knelt down in homage to him. After mocking him, they stripped him of the purple cloak and put his own clothes on him. Then they led him out to crucify him.

(Mark 15.15–20)

❖ Pilate took Jesus and had him flogged. And the soldiers wove a crown of thorns and put it on his head, and they dressed him in a purple robe. They kept coming up to him, saying, 'Hail, King of the Jews!' and striking him on the face.

(John 19.1–4)

Jesus Prayer
Jesus, Lord and Christ,
Son and Word of the Living God:
you were despised and rejected,[33]
have mercy (on us).

Concluding Prayer
Lord God,
whose blessed Son our Saviour
gave his back to the smiters
and did not hide his face from shame:
give us grace to endure the sufferings of this present
    time
with sure confidence in the glory that shall be
    revealed;
through Jesus Christ our Lord.[34]

4 The Crucifixion of Jesus

(a) According to Mark: 'Those who passed by derided him'

[The soldiers] compelled a passer-by, who was coming in from the country, to carry [Jesus'] cross; it was Simon of Cyrene, the father of Alexander and Rufus. Then they brought Jesus to the place called Golgotha (which means the place of a skull). And they offered him wine mixed with myrrh;[35] but he did not take it. And they crucified him, and divided his clothes among them, casting lots to decide what each should take.

It was nine o'clock in the morning when they crucified him. The inscription of the charge against him read,
'The King of the Jews.' And with him they crucified two
bandits, one on his right and one on his left. Those who
passed by derided him, shaking their heads and saying,
'Aha! You who would destroy the temple and build it
in three days, save yourself, and come down from the
cross!' In the same way the chief priests, along with the
scribes, were also mocking him among themselves and
saying, 'He saved others; he cannot save himself. Let
the Messiah, the King of Israel, come down from the
cross now, so that we may see and believe.' Those who
were crucified with him also taunted him.

(Mark 15.21–32)

❖ He trusts in God; let God deliver him now, if he
wants to; for he said, 'I am God's Son.'

(Matthew 27.43)

Jesus Prayer
Jesus, Lord and Christ,
Son and Word of the Living God:
you loved me
and gave yourself up for me[36]
have mercy (on us)

Concluding Prayer

Thanks be to thee, our Lord Jesus Christ,
for all the benefits which thou hast given us,
for all the pains and insults which thou hast borne
   for us.
O most merciful Redeemer, Friend, and Brother,
may we know thee more clearly,
love thee more dearly,
and follow thee more nearly
now and for ever more. Amen.[37]

(b) According to Luke: 'Truly I tell you, today you will be with me in Paradise'

When they came to the place that is called The Skull, they crucified Jesus there with the criminals, one on his right and one on his left.[38] And they cast lots to divide his clothing. And the people stood by, watching; but the leaders scoffed at him, saying, 'He saved others; let him save himself if he is the Messiah of God, his chosen one!' The soldiers also mocked him, coming up and offering him sour wine, and saying, 'If you are the King of the Jews, save yourself!' There was also an inscription over him, 'This is the King of the Jews.'

One of the criminals who were hanged there kept deriding him and saying, 'Are you not the Messiah? Save yourself and us!' But the other rebuked him, saying, 'Do you not fear God, since you are under the same sentence of condemnation? And we indeed have been condemned justly, for we are getting what we deserve for our deeds, but this man has done nothing wrong.' Then he said, 'Jesus, remember me when you come into your kingdom.' He replied, 'Truly I tell you, today you will be with me in Paradise.'

(Luke 23.33–43)

❖ 'Jesus, remember me when you come into your kingdom' . . . 'Truly I tell you, today you will be with me in Paradise.'

Jesus Prayer
Jesus, Lord and Christ,
Son and Word of the Living God:
you loved me
and gave yourself up for me
have mercy (on us).

Concluding Prayer
Jesus, Lord and Christ,
you brought the repentant thief

from the shame of the cross
into the joy of your kingdom.
We confess our sins,
and, trusting in your mercy,
we pray that at our life's end,
you will bring us through the gates of paradise
   rejoicing.
We ask this of you
who live and reign with the Father
in the unity of the Holy Spirit,
one God for ever and ever. Amen.[39]

5 The Death of Jesus on the Cross

*(a) According to Mark: 'My God, my God, why
have you forsaken me?'*

When it was noon, darkness came over the whole land
until three in the afternoon. At three o'clock Jesus cried
out with a loud voice, *'Eloi, Eloi, lema sabachthani?'*
which means, 'My God, my God, why have you forsaken me?' When some of the bystanders heard it, they
said, 'Listen, he is calling for Elijah.' And someone ran,
filled a sponge with sour wine, put it on a stick, and
gave it to him to drink, saying, 'Wait, let us see whether

49

Elijah will come to take him down.' Then Jesus gave a loud cry and breathed his last. And the curtain of the temple was torn in two, from top to bottom. Now when the centurion, who stood facing him, saw that in this way he breathed his last, he said, 'Truly this man was God's Son!'

There were also women looking on from a distance; among them were Mary Magdalene, and Mary the mother of James the younger and of Joses, and Salome. These used to follow him and provided for him when he was in Galilee; and there were many other women who had come up with him to Jerusalem.

(Mark 15.33–44)

❖ Then Jesus gave a loud cry and breathed his last. And the curtain of the temple was torn in two, from top to bottom. Now when the centurion, who stood facing him, saw that in this way he breathed his last, he said, 'Truly this man was God's Son!'

Jesus Prayer
Jesus, Lord and Christ,
Son and Word of the Living God:
**you were crushed with sorrow
and covered in darkness,**[40]
have mercy (on us).

Concluding Prayer
Almighty God,
who in the passion of your blessed Son
made an instrument of painful death
to be for us the means of life and peace:
grant us so to glory in the cross of Christ
that we may gladly suffer for his sake;
who is alive and reigns with you,
in the unity of the Holy Spirit,
one God, now and for ever.[41]

(b) According to Luke: 'Father, into your hands I commend my spirit'

It was now about noon, and darkness came over the whole land until three in the afternoon, while the sun's light failed; and the curtain of the temple was torn in two. Then Jesus, crying with a loud voice, said, 'Father, into your hands I commend my spirit.'

Having said this, he breathed his last. When the centurion saw what had taken place, he praised God and said, 'Certainly this man was innocent.' And when all the crowds who had gathered there for this spectacle saw what had taken place, they returned home, beating their breasts. But all his acquaintances, including the women who had followed him from Galilee, stood at a distance, watching these things.

(Luke 23.44–49)

❖ Then Jesus, crying with a loud voice, said, 'Father, into your hands I commend my spirit.' Having said this, he breathed his last.

Jesus Prayer
Jesus, Lord and Christ,
Son and Word of the Living God:
**you gave yourself into the hands of the Father,
have mercy (on us).**

Concluding Prayer
Lord Jesus,
you were obedient to the point of death,
even death on a cross.[42]

Faithfulness to your Father's work[43]
has brought you to this hour.

May your Spirit so transform our lives
that the mind that was in you may also be in us.[44]
Then, at the last, your words will have become our
    own:
'Father, into your hands I commend my spirit.'[45]

We ask you this who live and reign with the Father
in the unity of the Holy Spirit,
for ever and ever. Amen.[46]

(c) According to John: 'When Jesus had received
the wine, he said "It is finished." Then he bowed his
head and gave up his spirit'

Meanwhile, standing near
the cross of Jesus were his
mother, and his mother's sister, Mary the wife of Clopas,
and Mary Magdalene. When
Jesus saw his mother and
the disciple whom he loved
standing beside her, he said
to his mother, 'Woman, here
is your son.' Then he said to
the disciple, 'Here is your

mother.' And from that hour the disciple took her into his own home.

After this, when Jesus knew that all was now finished, he said (in order to fulfil the scripture), 'I am thirsty.' A jar full of sour wine was standing there. So they put a sponge full of the wine on a branch of hyssop and held it to his mouth. When Jesus had received the wine, he said, 'It is finished.' Then he bowed his head and gave up his spirit.

(John 19.25–30)

❖ And just as Moses lifted up the serpent in the wilderness, so must the Son of Man be lifted up, that whoever believes in him may have eternal life.

(John 3.14–15)

Jesus Prayer
Jesus, Lord and Christ,
Son and Word of the Living God:
you passed from this world to the Father,[47]
have mercy (on us)

Concluding Prayer
Almighty God, whose Son our Saviour Jesus Christ was lifted high upon the cross that he might draw the whole world to himself: Mercifully grant that we,

who glory in the mystery of our redemption, may
have the grace to take up our cross and follow him:
who lives and reigns with you and the Holy Spirit,
one God, in glory everlasting. Amen.[48]

At the centrepiece, recite one of the following: **Jesus,
Saviour of the World,** *the* **Song of Zechariah** *(Luke
1.68–79),* **Mary's Song of Praise** *(Luke 1.46–55), the*
Song of Simeon *(Luke 2.29–32).*

Meditations on Life in Christ

For each Meditation:
Announce the title of the Meditation.
Read the Scripture text.
Pause for reflection.
Say the Lord's Prayer on the single bead.
Say the Jesus Prayer on each of the ten beads.
Say the Glory be to the Father . . .
Say the Concluding Prayer.

1 The Resurrection of Jesus

(a) According to Paul: 'He was raised on the third day in accordance with the scriptures, and appeared to Cephas, then to the twelve"

Now I should remind you, brothers and sisters, of the good news that I proclaimed to you, which you in turn received, in which also you stand, through which also you are being saved, if you hold firmly to the message that I proclaimed to you – unless you have come to believe in vain.

For I handed on to you as of first importance what I in turn had received: that Christ died for our sins in accordance with the scriptures, and that he was buried, and that he was raised on the third day in accordance with the scriptures, and that he appeared to Cephas, then to the twelve. Then he appeared to more than five hundred brothers  and sisters at one time, most of whom are still alive, though some have died. Then he appeared to James, then to all the apostles. Last of all, as to someone untimely born, he appeared also to me.

(1 Corinthians 15.1–8)

❖ Christ has been raised from the dead, as the first-fruits of all who have fallen asleep.

(1 Corinthians 15.20, NJB)

(b) According to Mark: 'He has been raised; he is not here. Look, there is the place they laid him'

When the Sabbath was over, Mary Magdalene, and Mary the mother of James, and Salome bought spices, so that they might go and anoint [Jesus]. And very early on the first day of the week, when the sun had risen, they went to the tomb. They had been saying to one another, 'Who will roll away the stone for us from the entrance to the tomb?' When they looked up, they saw that the stone, which was very large, had already been rolled back. As they entered the tomb, they saw a young man, dressed in a white robe, sitting on the right side; and they were alarmed. But he said to them, 'Do not be alarmed; you are looking for Jesus of Nazareth, who was crucified. He has been raised; he is not here. Look, there is the place they laid him. But go, tell his disciples and Peter that he is going ahead of you to Galilee; there you will see him, just as he told you.'

(Mark 16.1–7)

❖ [The] angel said to the women, 'Do not be afraid; I know that you are looking for Jesus who was crucified. He is not here; for he has been raised, as he said. Come, see the place where he lay. Then go quickly and tell his disciples, "He has been raised from the dead, and indeed he is going ahead of you to Galilee; there you will see him." This is my message for you.'

(Matthew 28.5–7)

❖ 'Why do you look for the living among the dead? He is not here, but has risen'.

(Luke 24.5)

Jesus Prayer
Jesus, Lord and Christ,
Son and Word of the Living God:
you are risen from the dead,
have mercy (on us).

Concluding Prayer
Almighty Father,
who in your great mercy gladdened the disciples
with the sight of the risen Lord:
give us such knowledge of his presence with us,
that we may be strengthened and sustained
by his risen life
and serve you continually in righteousness and truth;
through Jesus Christ your Son our Lord,
who is alive and reigns with you,
in the unity of the Holy Spirit,
one God, now and for ever. Amen.[49]

2 The Ascension of Jesus to the Father[50]

(a) According to John: 'I will take you to myself, so that where I am, there you may be also'

[Jesus said] 'Do not let your hearts be troubled. Believe in God, believe also in me. In my Father's house there are many dwelling-places. If it were not so, would I have told you that I go to prepare a place for you? And if I go and prepare a place for you, I will come again and will take you to myself, so that where I am, there you may be also.'

(John 14.1–3)

(b) According to Luke: 'While he was blessing them, he withdrew from them and was carried up, into heaven'

Jesus said to the disciples, 'These are my words that I spoke to you while I was still with you – that everything written about me in the law of Moses, the prophets, and the psalms must be fulfilled.' Then he opened their minds to understand the scriptures, and he said to them, 'Thus it is written, that the Messiah is to suffer and to rise from the dead on the third day, and that repentance and forgiveness of sins is to be proclaimed in his name to all nations, beginning from Jerusalem. You are witnesses of these things. And see, I am sending upon you what my Father promised; so stay here in the city until you have been clothed with power from on high.'

Then he led them out as far as Bethany, and, lifting up his hands, he blessed them. While he was blessing them, he withdrew from them and was carried up into heaven. And they worshipped him, and returned to Jerusalem with great joy; and they were continually in the temple blessing God.

(Luke 24.44–53)

Jesus Prayer
Jesus, Lord and Christ,
Son and Word of the Living God:
you dwell for ever in the Father's heart,[51]
have mercy (on us)

Concluding Prayer
O God, whose dearly beloved Son was, by thy mighty power, exalted that he might prepare a place in thy kingdom of glory for them that love thee: So lead and uphold us, O most merciful Lord, that we may both follow the holy steps of his life here upon earth, and may enter with him hereafter into thy everlasting rest; that where he is, we may also be; through the same Jesus Christ our Lord. Amen.[52]

3 The Holy Spirit: Gift of the Easter Jesus

(a) According to John: the Spirit of God comes to us through the Glorified Christ

On the last day, the great day of the [Feast of Shelters], Jesus stood and cried out:

> 'Let anyone who is thirsty come to me!
>
> Let anyone who believes in me come and drink!
>
> As scripture says, "From his heart shall flow streams of living water."'

He was speaking of the Spirit which those who believed in him were to receive; for there was no Spirit as yet because Jesus had not yet been glorified.

(John 7.37–39, NJB)[53]

(b) According to John: the Risen Lord gives the Spirit on Easter Sunday

In the evening of that same day, the first day of the week, the doors were closed in the room where the disciples were, for fear of the Jews. Jesus came and stood among them. He said to them, 'Peace be with you,' and, after saying this, he showed them his hands and his side. The disciples were filled with joy at seeing the Lord, and he said to them again, 'Peace be with you.

'As the Father sent me,
so am I sending you.'

After saying this he breathed on them and said:

'Receive the Holy Spirit.
If you forgive anyone's sins,
they are forgiven;
if you retain anyone's sins,
they are retained.'

(John 20.19–23, NJB)[54]

❖ But the Advocate, the Holy Spirit, whom the Father will send in my name, will teach you everything, and remind you of all that I have said to you.

(John 14.26)

(c) According to Luke: the Pentecost outpouring from Christ filled with the Spirit

When the day of Pentecost had come, they were all together in one place. And suddenly from heaven there came a sound like the rush of a violent wind, and it filled the entire house where they were sitting. Divided tongues, as of fire, appeared among them, and a tongue rested on each of them. All of them were filled with the Holy Spirit and began to speak in other languages, as the Spirit gave them ability.

Now there were devout Jews from every nation under heaven living in Jerusalem. And at this sound the crowd gathered and was bewildered, because each one heard them speaking in the native language of each. Amazed and astonished, they asked, 'Are not all these who are speaking Galileans? And how is it that we hear, each of us, in our own native language? . . . [In] our own languages we hear them speaking about God's deeds of power.'

(Acts 2.1–8, 11)

❖ Now raised to the heights by God's right hand, [Christ] has received from the Father the Holy Spirit, who was promised, and what you see and hear is the outpouring of that Spirit . . . For this reason the

whole House of Israel can be certain that the Lord
and Christ whom God has made is this Jesus . . .

(Acts 2.33, 36, NJB)

❖ Those who are led by God's Spirit are God's children. For the Spirit that God has given you does not
make you slaves and cause you to be afraid; instead,
the Spirit makes you God's children, and by the Spirit's power we cry out to God 'Father! my Father!'

(Romans 8.14–15, GNB[55])

Jesus Prayer
Jesus, Lord and Christ,
Son and Word of the Living God:
you share with us the life-giving Spirit,
have mercy (on us).

Concluding Prayer
Come, O Spirit of God,
and make within us your dwelling place and home.

May our darkness be dispelled by your light,
and our troubles calmed by your peace.

May all evil be redeemed by your love,
all pain transformed through the suffering of Christ,
and all dying glorified in his risen life. Amen.[56]

4 The Life of Grace

(a) In the Letter to the Ephesians: an outpouring of thanks for our union with Christ through the Spirit, the pledge of future glory

Let us give thanks to the God and Father of our Lord Jesus Christ! For in our union with Christ he has blessed us by giving us every spiritual blessing in the heavenly world.

Even before the world was made, God had already chosen us to be his through our union with Christ, so that we would be holy and without fault before him.

Because of his love God had already decided that through Jesus Christ he would make us his children – this was his pleasure and purpose.

Let us praise God for his glorious grace, for the free gift he gave us in his dear Son! For by the sacrificial death[57] of Christ we are set free, that is, our sins are forgiven. How great is the grace of God, which he gave to us in such large measure!

In all his wisdom and insight God did what he had purposed, and made known to us the secret plan he had already decided to complete by means of Christ. This plan, which God will complete when the time is right, is to bring all creation together, everything in heaven and on earth, with Christ as head.

All things are done according to God's plan and decision; and God chose us to be his own people in union with Christ because of his own purpose, based on what he had decided from the very beginning.

Let us, then, who were the first to hope in Christ, praise God's glory!

And you also became God's people when you heard the true message, the Good News that brought you salvation. You believed in Christ, and God put his stamp of ownership on you by giving you the Holy Spirit he had promised. The Spirit is the guarantee that we shall receive what God has promised his people, and this assures us that God will give complete freedom to those who are his. Let us praise his glory!

(Ephesians 1.3–14, GNB)

Jesus Prayer
Jesus, Lord and Christ,
Son and Word of the Living God:
you are our freedom
and our hope of glory,
have mercy (on us).

Concluding Prayer
Almighty God,
by whose grace alone we are accepted
and called to your service;
strengthen us by your Holy Spirit
and make us worthy of our calling;
through Jesus Christ our Lord,
who is alive and reigns with you,
in the unity of the Holy Spirit,
one God, now and for ever.[58]

*(b) In the Letter to the Philippians: we break with
the past and reach out to the future with Christ*

I want to know Christ and the power of his resurrection
and the sharing of his sufferings by becoming like him
in his death, if somehow I may attain the resurrection
from the dead.

Not that I have already obtained this or have already reached the goal but I press on to make it my own, because Christ Jesus has made me his own. Beloved, I do not consider that I have made it my own; but this one thing I do: forgetting what lies behind and straining forward to what lies ahead, I press on towards the goal for the prize of the heavenly call of God in Christ Jesus.

(Philippians 3.10–14)

❖ This one thing I do: forgetting what lies behind and straining forward to what lies ahead, I press on towards the goal for the prize of the heavenly call of God in Christ Jesus.

(Philippians 3.13–14)

Jesus Prayer
Jesus, Lord and Christ,
Son and Word of the Living God:
you bear us into life,
have mercy (on us)

Concluding Prayer
Almighty and everlasting God,
increase in us your gift of faith
that, forsaking what lies behind
and reaching out to that which is before,

we may run the way of your commandments
and win the crown of everlasting joy;

through Jesus Christ your Son our Lord,
who is alive and reigns with you,
in the unity of the Holy Spirit,
one God, now and for ever. Amen.[59]

*(c) In the Letter to the Romans: the love of God is
ours through Jesus Christ our Lord*

If God is for us, who can be against us? Certainly not
God, who did not even keep back his own Son, but offered him for us all! He gave us his Son – will he not
also freely give us all things? Who will accuse God's
chosen people? God himself declares them not guilty!
Who, then, will condemn them? Not Christ Jesus, who
died, or rather, who was raised to life and is at the right
side of God, pleading with him for us! Who, then, can
separate us from the love of Christ? Can trouble do it,
or hardship or persecution or hunger or poverty or dan-
ger or death? No, in all these things we have complete
victory through him who loved us! For I am certain that
nothing can separate us from his love: neither death nor
life, neither angels nor other heavenly rulers or pow-

ers, neither the present nor the future, neither the world above nor the world below – there is nothing in all creation that will ever be able to separate us from the love of God which is ours through Christ Jesus our Lord.

(Romans 8.31–39, GNB)

❖ For I am certain that nothing can separate us from [God's] love: neither death nor life, neither angels nor other heavenly rulers or powers, neither the present nor the future, neither the world above nor the world below – there is nothing in all creation that will ever be able to separate us from the love of God which is ours through Christ Jesus our Lord.

(Romans 8.38–39, GNB)

Jesus Prayer
Jesus, Lord and Christ,
Son and Word of the Living God:
**you uphold us by your grace,
have mercy (on us).**

Concluding Prayer
O God, the protector of all who trust in you,
without whom nothing is strong, nothing is holy:
increase and multiply upon us your mercy;
that with you as our ruler and guide

we may so pass through things temporal
that we lose not our hold on things eternal;
grant this, heavenly Father,
for our Lord Jesus Christ's sake,
who is alive and reigns with you,
in the unity of the Holy Spirit,
one God, now and for ever. Amen.[60]

5 The New Jerusalem

(a) According to the Revelation to John

Then I saw a new heaven
and a new earth; for
the first heaven and the
first earth had passed
away, and the sea was
no more. And I saw the
holy city, the new Jeru-
salem, coming down
out of heaven from God
. . . And I heard a loud
voice from the throne
saying,

'See, the home of God is among mortals.
He will dwell with them;
they will be his peoples,
and God himself will be with them;
he will wipe every tear from their eyes.
Death will be no more;
mourning and crying and pain will be no more,
for the first things have passed away.'

And the one who was seated on the throne said, 'See, I am making all things new.' Also he said, 'Write this, for these words are trustworthy and true.' Then he said to me, 'It is done! I am the Alpha and the Omega, the beginning and the end. To the thirsty I will give water as a gift from the spring of the water of life. Those who conquer will inherit these things, and I will be their God and they will be my children.'

(Revelation 21. 1–7)

❖ And I heard a loud voice from the throne saying, 'See, the home of God is among mortals. He will dwell with them; they will be his peoples, and God himself will be with them; he will wipe every tear from their eyes. Death will be no more; mourning and crying and pain will be no more, for the first things have passed away.' And the one who was seated on the throne said, 'See, I am making all things new.'

(b) In the Letter to the Hebrews

You have not come to something that can be touched, a blazing fire, and darkness, and gloom, and a tempest, and the sound of a trumpet, and a voice whose words made the hearers beg that not another word be spoken to them . . . But you have come to Mount Zion and to the city of the living God, the heavenly Jerusalem, and to innumerable angels in festal gathering, and to the assembly of the firstborn who are enrolled in heaven, and to God the judge of all, and to the spirits of the righteous made perfect, and to Jesus, the mediator of a new covenant . . . Therefore, since we are receiving a kingdom that cannot be shaken, let us give thanks, by which we offer to God an acceptable worship with reverence and awe . . .

(Hebrews 12.18–19, 22–24a, 28)

❖ For we have not here a lasting city: but we seek one that is to come.

(Hebrews 13.14)

Jesus Prayer
Jesus, Lord and Christ,
Son and Word of the Living God:
you are the Alpha and the Omega,
the first and the last,
the beginning and the end,[61]
have mercy (on us)

Concluding Prayer
Almighty God,
you have made us for yourself,
and our hearts are restless till they find rest in you;
pour your love into our hearts and draw us to
    yourself,
and so bring us at last to your heavenly city
where we shall see you face to face;

through Jesus Christ your Son our Lord,
who is alive and reigns with you,
in the unity of the Holy Spirit,
one God, now and for ever. Amen.[62]

At the centrepiece, recite one of the following: **Jesus,**
Saviour of the World, *the* **Song of Zechariah** *(Luke*
1.68–79), **Mary's Song of Praise** *(Luke 1.46–55), the*
Song of Simeon *(Luke 2.29–32).*

Centrepiece Prayers

The Song of Zechariah[63]

Blessed be the Lord, the God of Israel,
for he has come to his people and set them free.

He has raised up for us a mighty Saviour,
born of the house of his servant, David.

Through his holy prophets, he promised of old
that he would save us from our enemies,
from the hands of all that hate us.

He promised to show mercy to our forebears,
and to remember his holy covenant.

This was the oath he swore to our father, Abraham,
To set us free from the hands of our enemies,

Free to worship him without fear,
holy and righteous in his sight,
all the days of our life.

You, my child,
shall be called the prophet of the Most High,
for you will go before the Lord to prepare his way,

To give his people knowledge of salvation
by the forgiveness of all their sins.

In the tender compassion of our God
the dawn from on high shall break upon us,

To shine on those who dwell in darkness
and the shadow of death,
and to guide our feet into the way of peace.

Glory be to the Father,
and to the Son,
and to the Holy Spirit,
One God, for ever and ever. Amen.

The Song of Mary[64]

My soul proclaims the greatness of the Lord,
my spirit rejoices in God my Saviour,

For he has looked with favour on his lowly servant.
From this day all generations will call me blessed.

The Almighty has done great things for me
And holy is his name.

He has mercy on those who fear him
in every generation.

He has shown the strength of his arm
he has scattered the proud in their conceit.

He has cast down the mighty from their thrones,
and has lifted up the lowly.

He has filled the hungry with good things,
and the rich he has sent away empty.

He has come to the help of his servant, Israel
for he has remembered his promise of mercy,

The promise he made to our forebears,
to Abraham and his children for ever.

Glory be to the Father,
and to the Son,
and to the Holy Spirit,
One God, for ever and ever. Amen.

The Song of Simeon[65]

Now, Lord, you let your servant go in peace;
your word has been fulfilled.

My own eyes have seen the salvation
which you have prepared in the sight of every
   people:
a light to reveal you to the nations
and the glory of your people Israel.

Glory be to the Father,
and to the Son,
and to the Holy Spirit,
One God, for ever and ever. Amen.

Jesus, Saviour of the World[66]

Jesus, Saviour of the world,
come to us in your mercy:
we look to you to save and help us.

By your cross and your life laid down,
you set your people free:
we look to you to save and help us.

When they were ready to perish,
you saved your disciples:
we look to you to come to our help.

In the greatness of your mercy,
loose us from our chains,
forgive the sins of all your people.

Make yourself known
as our saviour and mighty deliverer;
save and help us that we may praise you.

Come now and dwell with us, Lord Christ Jesus;
hear our prayer and be with us always.

And when you come in glory,

make us to be one with you
and to share the life of your kingdom.

Glory be to the Father,
and to the Son,
and to the Holy Spirit,
One God, for ever and ever. Amen.

Jesus, Saviour of the world,
come to us in your mercy:
we look to you to save and help us.

The General Thanksgiving

Almighty God, Father of all mercies,
we, your unworthy servants
give you most humble and hearty thanks
for all your goodness and loving-kindness.

We bless you for our creation, preservation
and all the blessings of this life;
but above all for your immeasurable love
in our Lord Jesus Christ,
for the means of grace and for the hope of glory.

And give us we pray
such a sense of all your mercies
that our hearts may be unfeignédly thankful,
and that we may show forth your praise,
not only with our lips but in our lives,
by giving up ourselves to your service,
and walking before you,
in holiness and righteousness, all our days;

through Jesus Christ our Lord,
to whom with you and the Holy Spirit,
be honour and glory,
for ever and ever. Amen.[67]

Appendix 1
The Jesus Clause when the 'Hail Mary' is Used

In the recitation of the Marian rosary, the following has been the custom for some time now. It was encouraged by Popes Paul VI and John Paul II. They referred to 'the custom in certain regions of highlighting the name of Christ by the addition of a clause referring to the mystery being contemplated'.[68] John Paul II saw it as a way of counteracting the effects of 'hurried recitation' and called it 'a praiseworthy custom, especially during public recitation . . . It is at once a profession of faith and an aid in concentrating our meditation . . .'[69] Some people do this on each of the nine beads, only adding the second part of the Hail Mary on the tenth: Holy Mary Mother of God, pray for us sinners now and at the hour of our death.

Meditations on the Infancy According to St Luke

Hail Mary,
full of grace.
The Lord is with thee.
Blessed art thou among women.
And blessed is the fruit of thy womb, Jesus,

– who is the work of the Holy Spirit.

– who comes to us like the dawn from on high.

– who is the image of the invisible God.

– who is a light to the gentiles
and glory to Israel.

– who was found in his Father's house.

Meditations on the Ministry

– who was anointed with the Holy Spirit and with
power.

– who changed the water into wine.

– who heals the broken-hearted
and binds up all their wounds.

– who was revealed in glory on the holy mountain.

– who is the bread of life.

Meditations on the Passion

– who abandoned himself to the will of the Father.

– who was given up into the hands of sinners.

– who was a man of sorrows and acquainted with grief.

– who bore our pain and carried our sorrows.

– who passed from this world to the Father.

Meditations on Life in Christ

– who was raised from the dead by the glory of God the Father.

– who dwells for ever in the heart of the Father.

– who shares with us the promise of the Holy Spirit.

– who calls us to the fullness of life.

– who is the Alpha and Omega,
the beginning and the end.

Appendix 2
Some Concluding Prayers

The following could be used after the Centrepiece Prayers.

Morning
As we reflect on your holy Word,
during this coming day Lord,
may we be enlightened by you,
the true light and source of all light.
We ask this through our Lord Jesus Christ your Son
who lives and reigns with you
in the unity of the Holy Spirit,
one God for ever and ever. Amen.[70]

Evening
Stay with us Lord Jesus,
because it is towards evening
and the day is now far spent.

As our companion along the way,
revive our hearts
and fill them with hope.

May we come to know you in the Scriptures
and in the breaking of bread.

We ask this of you
who live and reign with the Father
in the unity of the Holy Spirit,
one God for ever and ever. Amen.[71]

Night
Be present, O merciful God,
and protect us through the silent hours of this night,
so that we who are wearied by the changes
and chances of this fleeting world,
may rest upon your eternal changelessness;
through Jesus Christ our Lord. Amen.[72]

or:

Keep watch, dear Lord,
with those who wake, or watch or weep this night,
and give your angels charge over those who sleep.
Tend the sick,
give rest to the weary,

sustain the dying, calm the suffering,
and pity the distressed;
all for your love's sake, O Christ our Redeemer.
Amen.[73]

Appendix 3
Other Meditations

Meditating on the Heart of Jesus

On the last day, the great day of the [Feast of Shelters],
Jesus stood and cried out:

> 'Let anyone who is thirsty come to me!
> Let anyone who believes in me come and drink!
> As scripture says, "From his heart shall flow streams
> of living water."'

He was speaking of the Spirit which those who believed in him were to receive; for there was no Spirit as yet because Jesus had not yet been glorified.

(John 7.37–39, NJB)

It was the Day of Preparation, and to avoid the bodies' remaining on the cross during the Sabbath, since that Sabbath was a day of special solemnity, the Jews asked Pilate to have the legs broken and the bodies taken away. Consequently the soldiers came and broke the legs of the first man who had been crucified with [Jesus] and then of the other. When they came to Jesus, they saw he was already dead, and so instead of breaking his legs one of the soldiers pierced his side with a lance; and immediately there came out blood and water. This is the evidence of one who saw it, true evidence, and he knows that what he says is true, and he gives it so that you may believe as well. Because all this happened to fulfil the words of scripture:

Not one bone of his will be broken;
and again, in another place scripture says:
They will look to the one whom they have pierced.

(John 19.31–37, NJB)

❖ [At that time, Jesus said,] 'Come to me, all you that are weary and are carrying heavy burdens, and I will give you rest. Take my yoke upon you, and learn from me; for I am gentle and humble in heart, and you will find rest for your souls. For my yoke is easy, and my burden is light'.

(Matthew 11.28–30)

Jesus Prayer
Jesus, Lord and Christ,
Son and Word of the Living God:
you are all kindness and compassion,[74]
have mercy (on us).

Concluding Prayer
O God, whose bounty is infinite,
and whose tender compassion never fails:
fix our eyes on the heart of your Christ,
pierced for us on the cross,
and help us to recognize there
the sublime and boundless riches of your love.

Renewed by the power of your Spirit,
may we proclaim to others
the love of Christ that surpasses knowledge
and gladly share with them the treasure of
    redemption.

We ask this through our Lord Jesus Christ, your
    Son,
who lives and reigns with you
in the unity of the Holy Spirit,
God for ever and ever. Amen.[75]

Meditating on the Name of Jesus[76]

This is how Jesus Christ came to be born. His mother
Mary was betrothed to Joseph; but before they came to
live together she was found to be with child through the
Holy Spirit. Her husband Joseph, being an upright man
and wanting to spare her disgrace, decided to divorce
her informally. He had made up his mind to do this
when suddenly the angel of the Lord appeared to him
in a dream and said, 'Joseph son of David, do not be
afraid to take Mary home as your wife, because she has
conceived what is in her by the Holy Spirit. She will give
birth to a son and you must name him Jesus, because
he is the one who is to save his people from their sins.'
Now all this took place to fulfil what the Lord had spoken through the prophet:

Look! the virgin is with child
and will give birth to a son

whom they will call Immanuel,

a name which means 'God-is-with-us'.

(Matthew 1.18–23, NJB)

Jesus Prayer
Jesus, Lord and Christ,
Son and Word of the Living God:
you are Saviour and Emmanuel:
have mercy (on us).

Concluding Prayer
Lord, you have appointed your only begotten Son to
be the saviour of the human race and you have given
him the name of Jesus; grant in your goodness that
we, who venerate his holy name on earth, may also
enjoy the sight of him in heaven. We ask this in the
name of him who lives and reigns with you in the
unity of the Holy Spirit, one God forever and ever.
Amen.[77]

In Honour of St Benedict

Listen, child of God, to the guidance of your teacher.
Attend to the message you hear and make sure that it
pierces to your heart, so that you may accept with will-

ing freedom and fulfil by the way you live the directions that come from your loving Father. It is not easy to accept and persevere in obedience, but it is the way to return to Christ, when you have strayed through the laxity and carelessness of disobedience. My words are addressed to you especially, whoever you may be, whatever your circumstances, who turn from the pursuit of your own self-will and ask to enlist under Christ, who is Lord of all, by following him through taking to yourself that strong and blessed armour of obedience which he made his own on coming into our world . . .

However late, then, it may seem, let us rouse ourselves from lethargy. That is what scripture urges on us when it says: the time has come for us to rouse ourselves from sleep (Rom. 13.11). Let us open our eyes to the light that can change us into the likeness of God. Let our ears be alert to the stirring call of his voice crying to us every day: today, if you should hear his voice, do not harden your hearts (Ps. 94 [95].8). And again: let anyone with ears to hear listen to what the Spirit says to the churches (Rev. 2.7). And this is what the Spirit says: Come my children, hear me, and I shall teach you the fear of the Lord (Ps. 33 [34].11). Run, while you have the light of life, before the darkness of death overtakes you (Jn. 12.35).[78]

or:

[You] know the time has come for you to wake up from your sleep. For the moment when we will be saved is closer now than it was when we first believed. The night is nearly over, day is almost here. Let us stop doing the things that belong to the dark, and let us take up the weapons for fighting in the light . . . take up the weapons of the Lord Jesus Christ, and stop paying attention to your sinful nature and satisfying its desires.

(Ephesians 13.12, 14, GNB)

Jesus Prayer
Jesus, Lord and Christ,
Son and Word of the Living God:
you call us to return to you,
have mercy (on us).

Concluding Prayer
Eternal God,
who made Benedict a wise master
in the school of your service
and a guide to many called into community to `
    follow the rule of Christ:
grant that we may put your love before all else
and seek with joy the way of your commandments;
through Jesus Christ your Son our Lord,
who is alive and reigns with you,
in the unity of the Holy Spirit,
one God now and for ever.[79]

Notes

Meditations on the Infancy According to St Matthew

1 Collect for the Festival of St Joseph of Nazareth, *Alternative Service Book 1980* (Clowes, SPCK, Cambridge University Press, 1980), p. 760. From hereon, abbreviated ASB1980.

2 Collect for the Epiphany, *Celebrating Common Prayer* (London: Mowbray, 1992) p. 358. From hereon, abbreviated CCP.

3 'The *flight into Egypt* and the massacre of the innocents make manifest the opposition of darkness to the light: "He came to his own home, and his own people received him not" (Jn. 1.11). Christ's whole life was lived under the sign of persecution. His own share it with him (John 15.20). Jesus' departure from Egypt recalls the exodus and presents him as the definitive liberator of God's people (Matt. 2.15; Hos. 11.1)' (*Catechism of the Catholic Church* (London: Geoffrey Chapman, 1999), no. 530. From hereon, abreviated CCC.

4 Luke 2.34.

5 Author's own composition.

6 Luke 13.34.

7 Collect for the Festival of the Holy Innocents, ASB1980, p. 822.

8 Hosea 11.1.

99

9 Hebrews 2.10.

10 Author's own composition.

Meditations on the Infancy According to St Luke

11 Author's free rendering of the Latin Collect for 20 December, *Liturgia Horarum* I (Libreria Editrice Vaticana, 2000), p. 303.

12 Collect for the Festival of the Annunciation of the Lord, *Common Worship Daily Prayer* (London: Church House Publishing, 2005), p. 461. From hereon, abbreviated CWDP.

13 Luke 1.78.

14 Collect for the Festival of the Visit of the Blessed Virgin Mary to Elizabeth,
CWDP, p. 473.

15 Collect for the Festival of the Birth of the Blessed Virgin Mary, CWDP, p. 498.

16 Luke 2.31–32.

17 Collect for the Festival of the Presentation of Christ in the Temple, ASB1980, p. 757.

18 Author's own composition.

Meditations on the Ministry

19 Acts 10.38.

20 Author's own composition.

21 *Contemporary Parish Prayers*, compiled and edited by Frank Colquhoun (London: Hodder & Stoughton, 1975) prayer no. 59, p. 32.

22 Psalm 147.3.

23 Collect for the Fifth Sunday in Ordinary Time (B), *Opening Prayers*, (Norwich: Canterbury Press, 1997), p. 64.

24 Exodus 13.21.

25 Hebrews 1. 3.

26 2 Corinthians 3.18.

27 Author's own composition.

28 Luke 24.35.

29 1 Corinthians 10.16.

30 Author's own composition, based on *O Sacrum Convivium*, the Magnificat Antiphon from the Second Vespers of the Solemnity of the Body and Blood of Christ (*Liturgia Horarum, iuxta Ritum Romanum*, III (Libreria Editrice Vaticana MM) p. 542. From hereon, abbreviated LH III.

31 David F. Fleming, *The Spiritual Exercises of St Ignatius* (St Louis: The Institute of Jesuit Sources, 1978), p. 141.

32 Collect for Good Friday, CWDP, p. 427.

33 Isaiah 53.3.

34 Collect for Pentecost 13, ASB1980, p. 698.

35 A sedative, to mitigate the pain.

36 Galatians 2.20.

37 St Richard of Chichester (1197–1253), *Parish Prayers,* compiled and edited by Frank Colquhoun (London: Hodder & Stoughton, 1976), p. 61.

38 See NRSV margin note c at this point.

39 Author's free rendering of the Latin Collect for Friday None, Week 3, LH III, pp. 959–60.

40 Psalm 44.19.

41 Collect for Holy Cross Day, CWDP, p. 499.

42 Philippians 2.8.

43 Luke 2.49.

44 Philippians 2.5.
45 Luke 23.46.
46 Author's own composition.
47 John 13.1.
48 Collect for Holy Cross Day, *The Book of Common Prayer, According to the use of the Episcopal Church* (New York: Seabury Press, 1979), p. 244.

Meditations on Life in Christ

49 Collect for the Third Sunday of Easter, CWDP, p. 430.
50 It 'would be a misunderstanding of the Ascension if some sort of temporary absence of Christ from the world were to be inferred from it. The "sitting on the right hand of the Father" . . . signifies rather the human Jesus' participation in the kingly power of God, and so precisely his authoritative presence in the world and among those he has made his own . . . What the Ascension tells us about heaven is that it is the dimension of the divine and human fellowship, which is based on the resurrection and exaltation of Jesus. Henceforth, it designates the "place" (in the strictly ontological sense) in which man can live eternal life. Thus the Christian is aware that even in the present time his true life is hidden in "heaven" (Col. 3:3) because, by believing in Christ, he has entered into the dimension of God, and so, already in the here and now, into his own future' (Joseph Ratzinger, 'Ascension of Christ', *Sacramentum Mundi*, vol. 1, ed. A. Darlap (London: Burns & Oates, 1968), pp. 109–10).
51 John 1.18.
52 *Parish Prayers*, p. 99.

53 'The return to the Father upon which the sending of the Spirit depends is more than merely a change of place, it is a divinizing transformation (John 17.5) effected in Christ's death and resurrection . . . Christ must be exalted in his flesh into the glory of the Father in order for the rivers to flow from [him]' (F. X. Durrwell, *The Resurrection* (London and New York: Sheed and Ward, 1960), pp. 90–1).

54 'The authority conveyed implies an *extension of the ministry of Jesus through that of the Holy Spirit*. Jesus . . . gave sight, and faith, to the blind man who knew he was blind; to those who arrogantly claimed, "We see", he could say only, "Your sin remains" . . . For the work of the Spirit . . . perpetuates the ministry of Jesus, and when he convicts of unbelief he convicts of sin, since the relation of men to Christ determines their relation to God. This joint work, of Christ in sending the Holy Spirit and of the Holy Spirit in bearing witness to Christ is exercised in and through the church as represented by the disciples' (C. K. Barrett, *The Gospel According to St John* (London: SPCK, 1978), p. 571, emphases mine).

55 GNB: Good News Bible (London: The Bible Societies/HarperCollins, 1994).

56 A Collect for Monday Night Prayer, CCP, p. 61.

57 Marginal reading in GNB.

58 Collect for the Fifth Sunday Before Lent, CWDP, p. 421.

59 Collect for the Eighteenth Sunday After Trinity, CWDP, p. 441.

60 Collect for the Fourth Sunday After Trinity, CWDP, p. 436.

61 Revelation 22.13.

62 Collect for the Seventeenth Sunday after Trinity, CWDP, p. 441.

Centrepiece Prayers

63 CCP, p. 215.
64 CCP, p. 213.
65 CCP, p. 216.
66 CCP, p. 237.
67 CCP, p. 247.

Appendix 1: The Jesus Clause when the 'Hail Mary' is Used

68 John Paul II, *Rosarium Virginis Mariae*: Apostolic Letter on the Most Holy Rosary (London: Catholic Truth Society, 2002), no. 33.

69 *Rosarium Virginis Mariae*, no. 33.

Appendix 2: Some Concluding Prayers

70 Author's free rendering of the Latin Collect for Thursday Lauds, Week 2, LH III, p. 806.

71 Author's free rendering of the Latin Collect for Monday Vespers, Week 4, LH III, p. 1019.

72 Collect for Monday Night Prayer, CCP, p. 61.

73 Collect for Thursday Night Prayer, CWDP, p. 346.

74 Exodus 34.6.

75 Collect for the Sacred Heart of Jesus, *Prayers for Sundays and Seasons, Year B* (Chicago: Liturgy Training Publications, 1996), p. 150.

76 'But the one name that contains everything is the one that the Son of God received in his incarnation: JESUS. The divine name may not be spoken by human lips, but by assuming our humanity the Word of God hands it over to us and we can invoke it: "Jesus," "YHWH saves." The name "Jesus" contains all: God and man and the whole economy of creation and salvation. To pray "Jesus" is to invoke him and to call him within us. His name is the only one that contains the presence it signifies. Jesus is the Risen One, and whoever invokes the name of Jesus is welcoming the Son of God who loved him and who gave himself up for him' (CCC, no. 2666).

77 Collect for the Feast of the Holy Name of Jesus, *Saint Andrew Daily Missal* (Bruges: Abbey of St Andrew, 1959), p. 97.

78 Excerpts from the Prologue to the Rule of St Benedict, *The Benedictine Handbook* (Norwich: Canterbury Press, 2003) pp. 10–11.

79 Collect for the Festival of Benedict of Nursia, CWDP, p. 482.

Acknowledgements

Unless otherwise noted, scripture quotations are from the New Revised Standard Version of the Bible (NRSV), Anglicized Edition © 1989, 1995, Division of Christian Education of the National Council of the Churches of Christ in the United States of America. Used by permission. All rights reserved. The abbreviation NJB indicates the New Jerusalem Bible, published and copyright © 1966, 1967 and 1968 by Darton, Longman and Todd Ltd and Doubleday, a division of Random House, Inc. and used by permission. The abbreviation GNB indicates the Good News Bible, published by The Bible Societies/HarperCollins, © American Bible Society.

Extracts from *The Alternative Service Book* and *Common Worship Daily Prayer* are copyright © The Archbishops' Council, 2000, and are reproduced by permission. Material from *Celebrating Common Prayer* and the *Catechism of the Catholic Church* is reproduced with the kind permission of International Continuum Publishing Group, as is also the quotation